MANIFESTATION OF WORDS TO BE

1st Edition

Zadina M. Cadyma-Renard

Writing into the Realms—

ISBN: 9798859103010
Cover Design by: Creative_Chaos_77
Printed in the United States of America

ACKNOWLEDGMENTS

I would first like to thank my Lord and Savior Jesus the Christ, for without him, none of this would be possible. I am so thankful for my Husband, Jelfkeegan Renard for standing by me through thick and thin, sickness and in health and for everything else. I love you sweetie. I'd also like to thank my children Zechariah and Safiyah for showing me the love of Christ. They are resilient children and love God with all of their heart, and for that, I am grateful.

To my Father and Mother, Zadih and Marie Renelle, I love you both for instilling in me the love of learning and for encouraging me to pursue my dreams. To my brothers and sisters, Patrick, Adha, Zadih Jr., and Mahamma, I thank you for supporting me in all that I do. There are many people that I would like to thank, but this book would not do them justice, to you all who have been by my family's side, I thank you and pray that God would open all of the doors of opportunity, blessings, and peace in your lives in Jesus' name, Amen

PREFACE

My background as a writer began at the age of fourteen years old over twenty years ago in Boston, MA where I am from. I began writing to express my innermost thoughts as I wondered about the social, political, and spiritual topics that had a profound effect on me during that time. (I am currently thirty-eight as of the publishing of this poetry book)

Most significantly, I started to write out of the sheer pain and experience of being a child of divorced parents. This particular book of poems displays my journey and transformation into my identity with Jesus the Christ. Having said that, I would like to think that as you read the poems, you will begin to see what my spiritual life was like before and after my encounter with Christ.

This is the beauty of Spiritual Transformation when the Holy Spirit inspires it. Till date, and through the last 25 years of my life, I have witnessed for myself, how God has transformed me and how he has redeemed my life. My prayer is that as you read my book of poems, that you too may be transformed by the renewing of your mind (Rom. 12:2).

CONTENTS

GOD GAVE LIFE TO A SAVED SINNER

God gave me life.
God gave me the breath of air.
The will to continue when failure appeared at every corner.
God gave me the strength to continue the journey.
God's mercy is what keeps me grounded when others have fallen.

Indeed, I was free when I received his Healing during the fight against dark principalities and not against the flesh.
God fought for me so that Jesus could seal the deal.
My life was bought and cannot be returned to someone who never owned it.

I once saw my body as damaged goods, not worthy of love, respect, and adoration.
Regarded as a harlot by many who called themselves Christians.

Regarded as a child of divorce.
Regarded as a post abortionist.
Regarded as the biggest sinner Alive
No... I am regarded as the Child of God, a child of the one who sent his only son to be sacrificed on the cross for the sins that you and I have committed.

My life is not my own, my life was saved for the ultimate price.
God has the deed to Zadina Musau Kadima, descendant from the House of Abraham, Ishmael, and the house of David. Selah.

THE POWER OF YOUR TEMPLE

Your temple may be the best thing that God has created
on this earth,
But it is not the only thing that God gave you to use.
You have the choice of using your mind power as a means
to knowledge.

You have the choice of using your mouth to strengthen
network relationships.
You have the choice to use your feet in exploring your
career options.

You have the choice to use your tongue in demonstrating
your ability to express your needs.
You have the choice to use your hands in writing what your
goals in life are.

You have the choice to use your fingers in flipping the
pages of your history.
You have the choice to curl your toes towards the floor in
discovering the next best opportunity.
You have the choice of sealing your lips to practice
patience but most importantly Godliness.

You have the choice of using your behind to be seated on
the chair of educators within your city and neighborhood.
Woman of God,
You have so much potential,
But yet you stay ignorant of the truth that stares you in
your face.

You know what you have to do, You know what must be
done, And you know what is necessary to survive, But you
fail to do what is necessary to be alive. Be the Queen that
you once were in realizing your highest majesty.

Be the woman that you always wanted to be,
But didn't have enough guts to be.
The power of the temple must only come at the moment of
maturity, And at an understanding of yourself.

The only way that the power of the temple will be a force to
reckon with,
Is when you decide that you want to bring in a new generation of
children, That will follow your positive actions.

When this takes place, Your king will realize the ultimate power of
your temple, And will fight other men in defense of his queendom.
Never underestimate the power of the temple, Because the
temple is only as valuable as the woman who holds it.

AWAKE

I lie here contemplating.
Calculating.
Conversating,
My confusion.
It's an illusion.
It's defusing my inner ability to think correctly.
It's profoundly insane, deep in my membrane.

My mind is abused, a victim of poetry it has become.
I'm escaping; I'm brutalizing a place of peace.
I am in turbulence.

I am no longer controlled.
My mind is now the stronghold.
I am finally alone.

I begin to drown in water, awakening from the past.
I am now free from my history.
I have been released from a spiritual sentence.
I have been freed from a crime done to thy soul.
I am no more a silence untold. I have awoken.

ENLIGHTENED AUTISM

You want to speak but I will not hear you,
I will listen.
You are told by others that you are disabled,
Mentally retarded,
Physically challenged,
"Crazy" or downright possessed,
but to me, you are nothing less
But blessed.

I was always confused about your state,
But as a human being, I can relate.
It was always a mystery if mom drank while she held you in her
womb, I realize now that the world is a universal tomb,
That you have been delivered from.

You are not in man's realm; you have been birthed in the spirit realm.
I thought; why are you not normal?
Why aren't you like the rest of us?
The frightening thing is, is that you are.
You are me.
You are us.

You are no more an unfound clue,
The world has disabled you.
There were times when tears expressed my love for you.
But forever more, My smile will symbolize your being to simple
minds.
You are seen as a burden to come as destruction.
In my eyes, You are the enlightened to bring forth the prophesied
construction of humanity.
I hurt because I am not with you every step of the way,
Believe me, sister, Never will I go astray.

Dedicated to my younger sister with Autism.

FATHER PROTECTOR

Father.
Father of my heart.
Father of God.
Father of Congo.
Father of me.
I look upon you like a star that shines in the black sky of my world.
My protector.
My guard.

Father, you are infinite in the realm of universal abundance.
You were persecuted.
Looked down upon.

Despite this,
You remain to maintain the aura of life.
Life within your spirit.
Life within your mind.
As I gaze in the mirror,
The reflection is of you.

Your eyes, my eyes.
Our eyes in one.
My father of prophecy,
Truth and light.

I TRY

I try hard to be different from her,
I try hard to be better.
I try hard to break the cycle of infidelity,
I try hard to be the nurturer she never was to me.
I try hard to balance the daddy-girl persona.
I try hard to be the woman that is positive.
I try hard to be the woman that respects her body,
Spirit and mind.
I try hard to be the woman that is respected.
I try hard to be the woman that keeps God closer to her heart,
And the men further away from her Southern Paris.

WHO I AM

Who am I to shrink my success?
Who am I not to take that risk?
Where does it say that I have to deem myself average?
I am beyond myself to deny my greatness.
As a child of God,
I walk with no foolish pride,
But with confidence in who I am,
And where I come from.

As a child of God,
When I walk,
the heads of people turn in awe of my aura.
This may be mistaken for overconfidence.
It is understandable that when confidence appears, fear arises.
For he who isn't aware of their self-worth,
Fears the one who is confident.

This philosophy of mine is experienced from day to day.
Who are you to question my self-worth?
Who are you to question my façade?
Decipher my character, and then you shall know who I am in
essence.
Decipher my compassion, and I will show you who I am.
Decipher my intentions, and I will lead you toward a self-worthy
path.

Do not follow me into destruction,
But lead me into your light.
I do not renounce darkness,
But use it as a shadow that soon reveals itself to the surface.
To find a means to an end to who I am does no justice for my
virtuosity.

YOU

You can't be corrupted internally,
And in turn corrupt others around you.
There needs to be Peace within you,
Before Peace with Humanity.

JOHN 14:27

"Peace, I leave with you, my peace I give unto you, not as the world giveth,
give I unto you. Let not your heart be troubled, neither let it be afraid."
My friends, peace is an awesome thing,
Peace is what keeps you when John, Ricky,
And Mike are calling.

Peace is what nurtures you,
When everything around you falls down in destruction.
Peace is what heals you, When the root of your childhood pain
returns to kill your destiny.
Peace is the substance of calm,
In the midst of chaos and confusion.
Peace is knowing that God saved you from misery and delivered you to
Joy.

Peace brethren, unto you he gave peace of mind,
And a piece of life in the spirit of the comforter.
As tears roll down my face as I call out his name,
I feel the peace of his arms holding me from mediocrity.
I feel the touch of his fingers caressing my dreams to fulfillment.
I can taste the intimacy of his heart bringing me to patience for
unconditional love.

This my friends is what peace is,
This peace keeps me from making temptation a reality.
This peace allows me to set apart reality from fantasy.
Peace is the only thing I know.
Peace is the only thing I want to know,
For misery has no name in my book.
PEACE. Selah.

MARRIAGE

In marriage, I sacrifice,
In marriage I crucify,
In marriage I need,
In marriage I share,
In marriage, I do not compare,
Marriage is complete.

Marriage lives not in deceit,
Marriage has no receipt,
Marriage hides nothing and shares all,
Marriage hates fear but expresses its fall.
Marriage is nothing without intent,
It is waist less in times of regret.
For marriage without two people,
Is a tragedy within itself.

Marriage with one person,
Is the apocalypse breathing no help.
Relationships fear intimate relations,
Relationships leave options for escaping.

My relationship pulled the rabbit out of the hat,
The magic act is in motion and there's no turning back.
Relationships are felt but are not witnesses,
Lust can rear its ugly head and can become your mistress.
Relations without marital consent are highly frowned upon,
But a marriage that ends in divorce,
Is the most common among all.

THE ASSET

In my unmarried state of mind,
God has chosen me to be single,
And whole in all of his glory.

He has chosen for us to seek his face in our singleness.
In your singleness, Your struggle is not being alone,
But your purpose is fellowship with God.
Seek to become the Asset that understands how to give.
Be the Asset that gives love,
And not the asset that is empty.

In my singleness, every day is a new journey with God
that I cherish.
Each day is an example of his awesomeness,
Because I know he comforts me,
When I'm tempted.

THE HUSBAND GOD WILL SEND ME WHEN I AM WHOLE

Must be in a relationship with God i.e., must be in Eden.
Must enjoy life for all it has to offer.
Must enjoy traveling.

Must take pride in appearance and hygiene.
Must have a desire to have 2-3 Children.
Must love what he does for a career.
Must have joy in his life.

Must have goals in his life.
Must be a family man.
Must be proud of his heritage.
Must be able to give.

Must be able to have an intellectual conversation.
Must have compassion.
Must honor his parents.
Must have a sense of humor.

ULTIMATE COMFORTER

Now I am beginning to understand.
Now I am beginning to see the purpose, behind your life for me.
For so long, I thought that if a man's arms were around me,
I was of value.
But it's a trick.

I said to you, That I needed you in my life as my Lord and Savior,
But my actions spoke otherwise.
I toiled in bed with the enemy,
And he told me that it felt good.

But what he didn't tell me,
Was that my spirit would be forfeited in the process.
He told me that this is all I needed to make it through the day,
But what he failed to say to me was that I'd be dead by sunrise.
Man! His arms felt good around my waist,
But I see now that my decision was made in haste.

I didn't trust God for his promise of intimacy,
And for his promise of unconditional love.
I am beginning to see now,
That I deserve all the fruits that God has promised me,
But without faith in him, the only thing left to do is to settle for less.

But I tell you that if I wait with and for God,
I can and will be blessed, for Jehovah Jireh is my ultimate comforter,
When I am longing for arms around my waist.

FREE LOVE PART II

What has our world come to?
What do we have to show for?
More evil?
More war?
More blood lust?
More bloodshed?
More suffering?
More racism?
More killing?
More discrimination?
Is that what we want?
More?
More of what we can't handle?
Hate takes so much,
Hate takes a fist,
But love...love isn't a muscle.
It's what we are born with.
It's in us,
Its fate.
Evil is free will.
Evil is a choice.
It's what brings noise.
Love is humanity. Love is you and me.

INDEED

Indeed, I have risen.
Indeed, I have heard.
Indeed, I have forgiven.
Breathe life, not death my brothas and sistahs.
Are you thinking?
Or are you fornicating verbal poison?

INTERNALLY

In the time of strife,
I fight the spiritual combat of demons, combined to defeat me.
Just leave me.
Every day is a war,
Against mankind.

Mankind in conflict with fallen angels,
I remain stable.
Not moved or deterred from the universal goal,
I'm forever a woman hear me roar.
Invincible to Satan's hate,
I stay awake.

I transcended from the simple to the complex.
As a man fall's victim to a seizure,
I wonder in my mind, should I leave him?
As he sits there trembling immensely,
It suddenly occurs to me,
I cry eternally for humanity.
I cry internally for the hate, and catastrophic plagues of the world.

I'm one woman hear me roar,
Never forget that we are at war.

WILL

What is death?
Death of evil?
Death of what hasn't even begun?
As taught,
In order to receive God in my heart,
It's necessary that self must die.

Not the spiritual,
But the physical self.
My will has to die, in turn for God's
will to intervene.
When one kills another,
It's his will, but to punish him with death
is not man's will,
but God's will.

Who are we to Judge?
Who are we to punish?
Who are we to condemn?
Death has endless faces.
Just one purpose.

AMEN

Will those who love the Lord say Amen?
Amen, Amen, Amen, and Amen?
The Bible is an opening to my Godliness.
Despite my infancy in the Word,
I aim to grow in the word every day.
My goal is to die by Christ when I awake,
And to live by Christ when I slumber.
For the Bible is the opening to my Godliness.
Whether on my knees, standing, sitting, or walking,
The word is my only salvation.
Because there is no other way.

When I've attempted to live in my flesh,
I've soon come to realize that there is no other path worthy of following,
Because if I am not healed, I am surely not free.
Therefore, children of Christ, I beseech you to encounter the
Bible in motion, For the Holy Spirit moves through you in action.

The Holy Spirit is not dormant,
But lives through you in conversation with the Word.
Thus, igniting your relationship with the Most High God.
Now will those who Love the Lord say Amen, Amen, Amen, and Amen?
In the Lord, I've come to witness my weaknesses,
And despite myself, I fight to stay in God's Presence.
Because there is no other way.

In sin, I Praise him, in my Weakness I Praise him,
in my Strength, I Praise him,
And in the War against worldly powers,
I Praise him. Simply because there is no other way.

As you encounter the Bible as a radical, be balanced and
open to the word, So that you may be at God's attention
without hesitation but with expectation.

For a closed heart and mind knows no growth but only
speculation. Will those who Love the Lord
say Amen, Amen, and Amen? I only bring you these
words as a child of God, And as a friend in Christ
for without him there is no Life.
Because simply put, there is no other way.

ANOINTING

In the presence of supernatural wisdom,
The hour of death is not forsaken.
Satan refuses our souls in fear of God's arrival within us.
Our spirits then do not suffer the isolation of the underworld.

If the will withholds strength,
Deceit is disintegrated into nothingness.
Disperse temporary craving and embrace the eternal weapon.
A shield without anointing is powerless.

GOD IS

There is an explosion of fire,
Deep from the throat of the known messiah.
I once had a reprobate mind not wanting to
follow the truth. I turned away from the creator
and to the creation.

I have learned that he is and not was.
In my spirit, God has revealed himself through
the prophetic of his word.

Within the word, Worship is what man uses to
battle spiritual warfare. For if not to magnify God,
You magnify being. For in this way,
I am aware of the presence beholding God in
the holy power. I once was and I became.
It is often said that if God loved us,
We would not be allowed to suffer.

Who are we to speak of such pride within fault?
In the beginning, it was intended for us to
experience utopia. But from the weakness
of man, The pursuit of peace demands warfare.

And so it lives for eternity.
God never was and never became.
He is and remains infinite.

I SERVE

I serve as a muse to God,
I am a tool for his wonders.
He transports himself through me,
I am a metaphysical replica of his message.

I am his angel of communication,
Prepared for persecution by non-believers.
I serve as a soldier in the Army of Light.
My Amor is neither of Gold nor man-made.

But of his grace and fire.
His words through me,
Are intended for the physical realm,
Rooted from the spiritual.

LIKE HIM

Like the father,
He dreams of the vision.
Like the son,
She proclaims the vision,
And to the hand of the holy spirit, the vision is carried out.

As one can be true to the belief,
One can prophesy falsely,
And remain ignorant of the truth giving signs to the end of age.
Become aware of those preaching the good word,
And not God's word.
In light of not being misled,
My spirit bears witness to these words.
In wisdom, My personal prophecies have no time in themselves,
But God's timing element.

If I shall be judged,
I shall not be judged by being,
But by prophecy.
The tongue is as powerful as the actions that support it.
I am neither the prophet,
Nor the prophetess.
I am she who believes prophetically in what God proscribes as
medicine to the world.

I am neither perfect nor flawless,
But I remain humble and correctible to the doing of the Lord upon
me.

I am dependent on the spirit of truth,
And I am independent of the evil conspiracy.
I seek not of answers that have an end,
But of questions that have beginnings to solutions unsolved.

PROTECTION OF PURPOSE

Why are you here?
Where do you come from?
Where are you going?
Who are you?
What can you do?
Children of God,
Your Purpose is your protection,
Your Purpose is your reason,
Your meaning,
Your living,
And you're Glory.
It is the choice that you made to ensure it,
So, protect it,
Dream it,
Envision it,
See it,
Taste it,
Feel it,
Birth it.
It's your Purpose.
When you began,
God already established it.

He created it,
And all you have to do is chase it.
Children of God,
Run, don't walk,
Capture what you came here for.
The instructions that God gave you are simple: if you believe it, you can fulfill it.
For faith is not the substance seen,
But is the substance that is hoped for.

The Purpose that God has for you will prevail only if you allow his manual upon your life.
Speak it to receive it,
And take it to create it,
Because you are your destiny.
You are your paycheck,
And it's time to clock in because your lunch break is over.
Take your Gifts and apply them,
Because your Purpose is your protection.
Don't allow your funeral to be the resting place of your purpose,
Because your God-Given Purpose is your Protection.

Matthew 5:16 "Let your light so shine before men, that they may see your good works and glorify your Father which is in heaven..."
Children of God, you are part of a name brand called God Incorporated: THE WARNING LABEL READS: DON'T ROB THE EARTH OF YOUR PURPOSE!

SEARCHING

Finding,
Searching for an answer.
How can you?
When you don't know the question?
You roll on the floor,
Jump,
Hop,
Skip,
Flip,
And say God's name in vain.
How can you?
When you don't believe?
You will be forever searching.
Searching for what you know.
Acting as if you don't know.
Search,
Keep searching.
Search,
Keep searching.
The answer is there.
The answer is you.

STORM

In times of tribulation,
I look to God.
My human strength and self must die.
The power I feel is nothing fake but real.
The war against evil is never deceased but released,
To bring pure reincarnation in oneself.

In this Seventeenth year of life,
I give thanks to the testament of the word,
These truths have been revealed.
The first and the last: Revelation 1:4-8
"Grace and Peace to you from him who is,
And who was,
And who is to come.

And from the seven spirits before his throne,
And from Jesus Christ, who is the faithful witness, the firstborn
From the dead, and the ruler of the kings of the earth.

To him who loves us and has freed us from our sins by his blood;
And has made us to be a kingdom and priests to serve his God
And Father,
To him be the Glory and Power forever and ever!
Amen.

Look, he is coming with the clouds,
And every eye will see him,
Even those who pierced him,
And all the peoples of the earth will mourn because of him.
So shall it be!
Amen.

"I am the Alpha and the Omega,"
Says the Lord God,
"Who is, and who was,
And who is to come, the Almighty."
In my belief that this has come to pass,
Tears flow like the rain that washes my hair,
And like the rain that cleanses me of filth.
God poured his rainstorm in my eyes.

The storm of truths,
The storm of revelation,
The storm of a human nation.

THE COMING

The coming to Africa,
Will be likened to the prophesized coming of the
Lord on earth. Doomed is the man, who attempts,
To intervene against the word that annihilates all
evil.
Within its righteous path,
He who is above all in spirit is immune to
persecution,
But his flesh endures this persecution in the physical
realm of life.

In the core of Africa,
Lies a supernatural heartbeat of a nation,
That circulates the wisdom of 12,000 prophets,
Once known and now lost amongst the masses,
Of demons preparing for the destruction of a people.
She who is predestined for the greater purpose,
Will birth a revolution that had no era, but a given
time.

And so, it is written,
And so, it shall be done.
Within my conscious,
I'm not politically correct,
I'm poetically,
Biblically,
Historically,
Converting the confusion that confines us all.

To possess such accounts are against belief in its
self, Universal responsibility, Frees us from the
succession of wreaking havoc
Amongst mankind.

Our spiritual Armageddon has numbered our days
to imprisonment. Intertwining us within the state
of turmoil in the coming of he who is mighty,
The resurrection of these words shall come to
pass.

The demon crucifies to mortify.
The flesh unknowing that his soul has risen from
the purgatory, Brought forth cataclysms foretold
by intuition, Resulting in his ultimate
transcendence to prosperity.

WAITING AND WALKING

Thus says the lord.
Wait on him and he shall deliver,
Wait on him and he shall manifest,
Wait on him and you shall stand to inherit the best.

Walk away from that self-illusion,
Walk away to put behind that confusion.
Walk away into his refuge,
Walk away so that he can use you.
Walk away so that you can realize your true measure,
Walk away so that you can fulfill your higher potential.
Wait on him until you have mapped out a plan,
Wait on him to avoid building your house on sand.

Trust in him to provide your next course of action,
Believe in him and surely, he will make things happen.
Have faith in him for he shall provide a way,
Be grateful to him that you will live to see another day.
Confide in him with your most intimate thoughts,
Continue to worship him even when you are lost.
Be one with him,
For without oneness, the division shall be your demise.
Talk with him,
So that in your struggle you will discern with new eyes.
Cry to him,
For your tears serve as rain for a newfound gift.

Release your life to him,
So that you can begin to uplift.
Whether he chooses to speak with you through spirit, mind,
or soul, Remember that he created you and knows what you
behold.

MUSIC IN THE SPIRIT

The music in the spirit,
The spirit in the music,
Hallowed be thy name.
Lifting and moving from,
The source of which it came.
Take notice as his power moves through you.
Be aware that he came not to restrict you,
But to free you.

Your transgressions have been deleted,
Because of the flesh of his flesh,
And the blood of his blood,
And all it took was God's only begotten son.
So please take heed,
And understand your purpose,
Before planting the mustard seed.
You have been the chosen note,
To complete this composition.

The tune has been created.
Be the conductor that has no limit on his choir,
Be the director that orchestrates,
The timing of the act without care of criticism.
The music in the spirit,
The spirit in the music,
Taking back from the source of our power,
So that we can use it once more.

YOU'RE RESUME

It's not about what you've done;
It's about where you're going.
You see, the world requires your resume,
And only looks at what you've accomplished,
And in the process kills the potential that you have inside of you.
Don't you know that wherever there is creation,
God lives and breathes inside of you.
Wherever there is potential,
God manifests in you.

It's not about your resume,
It's about what you will do and shall do.
The next time you sit down at a job interview to prove your worth
to a man or woman, That knows not of your potential,
You tell him or her that you are in the essence
Of the Omni potent, most high God.

You tell them that you are the resume,
You tell them that you haven't seen anything yet,
Because there is so much more to come.
The resume that you look upon sits before you just waiting
to ignite its potential.

The resume that has yet to come when ignited,
Shall be Righteous, Effective, Saved, Undefiled, Magnificent, and
Elevated.
If you are a Child who hears this message as overconfidence,
Then I'm sorry to say that you haven't even begun to tap into your
potential.

Be not what is expected of you,
But be the product of fulfilling your potential.
This time has never been better,
Because your time is long overdue.
Be the resume that God created you to be,
Not the resume that has defined you to the world.

ABOUT THE AUTHOR

Zadina Musau Cadyma-Renard is a native of Boston, MA. She is also a mother and a wife of two beautiful and inquisitive children who she likes to call her Irish Twins. She is married to Jelfkeegan Renard, a native of Hinche Haiti.

Jelfkeegan Renard is also the founder of MARS International Ministries which is a Christian Organization that was created to commemorate his late mother; Marie Ange Samson-Renard for the purpose of helping those who are less fortunate in Haiti. The organization also ministers to the Haitian people both domestically and abroad to help lead them to Christs Salvation. Zadina and her family currently reside in Charlotte, NC where they have resided for the past 5 years.

Zadina is a graduate of Salem State University, class of 2007 and is also a graduate of Northeastern University, class of 2011. She is also an alum of the Boston Teacher Residency Program. Zadina speaks five languages, which includes English as a native speaker, Haitian Creole as her second language, French conversationally as her third language and has been learning Zulu and Swahili for the past year. She is also an avid Poet who has been writing poetry for the Glory of God for over 20 years and hopes to publish more books to give God the Glory.

Zadina was recently Ordained as a Minister through the Christian Leaders Alliance in addition to becoming an Ambassador for Christ through the Peacefire organization which is a 501c (3) organization with the mission of equipping people to respond to conflict as ambassadors of Jesus Christ.

When Zadina is not working Full time as an HR Professional within the Banking Industry, she can be found teaching Chair Zumba at Senior Living Facilities within the Greater Charlotte area. She is also a Group Fitness Instructor and enjoys working out on her Peloton from Home or walking at the track. She also enjoys learning about technology and computers and has recently completed a COMP TIA A+ Course at CPCC (Central Piedmont Community College).

Zadina can be found online on Facebook, Twitter, Instagram, and YouTube as Fearless for Christ where she leads her online ministry sharing more about her testimony and the goodness of God to help others say "Yes," to Jesus Christ so that they too can worship him in Spirit and in Truth.

Where you can Find the Author Online:
Facebook: Fearlessforchrist7
Instagram: Fearlessforchrist
Twitter: Fearless4jesus7
YouTube: Fearlessforchrist
https://www.soulcenters.org/directory/fruitful-garden-ministry-practice/
FruitfulGardenministry.org
Marsmissionaryoutreach.org
Vitalinvestmentsinc.com

www.ingramcontent.com/pod-product-compliance
Lightning Source LLC
Chambersburg PA
CBHW031434250726
48656CB00002B/990